Confessions of the Walker Stalker

How I Gave
America a Mobility Makeover
(With Sexy Canes and Turbo Hot Walkers)

Dedicated to my beautiful mother who told me to "write this down".

I finally listened.

Contents

Confessions of the Walker Stalker

Hello my name is Sue Chen and I am the Walker Stalker.

I've been a walker stalker for nearly two decades and I can't stop myself. I see someone using a broken down ugly cane, or patiently pushing a clumsy, gray walker — the kind with filthy tennis balls attached to the legs — and I have to follow. I have to stalk.

Or maybe it's the person, young or old, who is sitting weighed down in a wheelchair that is outdated and lackluster. Hospital gear. But is this person in a hospital? No. Prison, maybe. A terrible prison. The prison of lasting, unfair assumptions and discrimination. The prison of clunky medical equipment designed with all the flair and innovation that 18th Century technology can muster.

The product is so awful you can't help but feel uncomfortable. It's made for a hopeless condition, not an individual with personality and style. It's not made for the joyfully alive, it's made for people society ignores, believing they are dull and gray and dying, believing they are their equipment. Don't you hope this will never be you – defined by such institutional looking medical devices?

When I began stalking, the injustice often made me so frustrated. Then I'd get angry. People deserved better. My customers deserved better. Trade the tennis balls and rickety piece of "bent metal" - the actual industry term for a walker - for fashionable function and edgy trends. Customize with a favorite color and pattern. Consider red. Hot red! Consider leopard. Gucci, Chanel, Prada calling? Add your favorite turbo accessories. Yes, you can trick out your ride.

But what about the Gray Metal that has taken over United States mobility? How did this happen? How did I get here? How did I become the Walker Stalker? Well, it does go back to Gray...gray memories. Here are two.

My father Dr. Bruce Chen was a gifted rehabilitation doctor at the Veteran's Administration Center in Dublin, Georgia. I was nearly seven years old when I paid him a visit on campus to see what he really did for a living. Little did I know...

He was an action hero!

My dad gave his patients more than rehabilitation. No matter what their physical challenge, my dad found a way to improve their lives and give them hope. They lit up when they saw him because they knew he cared and had the unique power, gift and determination to help them feel whole again — despite physical challenges, inadequate walkers, wheelchairs and canes.

After a 13-year battle with cancer, my father passed away shortly after my 14th birthday. The day of his funeral is still a distinct memory, not a faded photograph. I went to the front of the church to play on my flute one of my dad's favorite pieces of music and saw at the back of the church, my dad's beautiful patients, there to support my family – with their gray pieces of bent metal.

They deserved better. The uniformly tawdry gear created a stigma that seemed to lump these amazing people into a caste of damaged and invisible people.

Not true! The patients my dad worked with

were incredible, unique individuals. They were brave and determined. They fueled a dream. My dad had a dream of providing independent living products that reflected the spirit and potential of the human beings he loved.

I didn't even know it at the time, but my dad's dream became a part of my soul and the Walker Stalker was born.

Ever since, I've developed a keen eye for mobility challenged people who would benefit from what I call The Mobility Makeover. I stalk them with my digital SLR or Flip video camera - not to disrupt them, but to help.   I glare, stare and follow...I approach with care and concern. I share and express that life can be fun, zesty and sexy with innovative, designer independent living products.

Live happy.
Live active.
Live well.
Live beautiful.

These are my messages.

My Walker Stalker Before and After images and confessions also help me prove my point to the world out there: medical equipment can be and must be as unique as the user.

Take action!   BE - As unique as you are!

Not all my memories are gray.   I have one that is in full living color. My childhood friend Christina Largetategi was twelve years old when she was thrown from a horse and suffered major head trauma. She was in a coma for more than a month. Her family feared that when she woke – if she woke - she would not be the same.

My father, who had only one more year to live,

told Christina's parents, "Your daughter will graduate school with my daughter Sue." After working intensively with my dad for months, Christina returned to classes the following year...and graduated with me. Completely Christina again.

Flash forward to our 20-year high school reunion. We both shed some tears when Christina recalled stopping me in the school hallway after her recovery and said, "Your father is the most wonderful man. He believed in me."

This is why I do what I do and why I will never stop: I am living my father's dream. I'm on a mission. I think he would be proud of his Walker Stalker.

Sue Chen
The Original Walker Stalker
Nova Founder and CEO

Be Warned!
Now entering a transformation zone

The purpose of The Mobility Makeover Handbook is to usher in a new era of independent living and personal style for people all over the world who are contending with physical challenges that affect their ability to live fully and independently.

My confessions herein constitute a revolution of awareness, aspirations, style, sensitivity — and solutions!

Brace yourself and be warned: Reading further may put you at risk of becoming a Walker Stalker. Should this occur you may experience pangs of compassion, fits of frustration, fury against injustice, sheer jubilation, as well as appreciation for what is most important in life – your personal mobility – because without it, you cannot go anywhere, do anything, see or be with anyone.

THERE IS NOTHING MORE IMPORTANT THAN YOUR PERSONAL MOBILITY.

Other symptoms you may experience:

- The sudden urge to follow people of all ages who may be struggling with ugly, inadequate walkers, wheelchairs and canes.

- Inquiring if you might suggest a Mobility Makeover strategy for the individuals you follow, including family members and neighbors, as well as complete strangers.

- Asking personal questions, such as What's your favorite color? Prefer an edgy pattern or a classic? Do you like to drive fast? Ever drink wine while … uh … relaxing in a hot tub with … uh … a friend?

- An obsessive need to see change happen NOW.

- A deep sense of satisfaction when observing the transformation of a fellow human being who realizes a red hot walker or leopard print cane can be as exciting as a new car or pair of sexy heels.

- Deep love for humanity and the amazing courage shown by others may also overwhelm and cause "happy" tears.

Before turning the page, please check the appropriate box.

☐ Yes, Sue, I am willing to risk all of the above so that I or someone I know or would like to know might live a better, more fulfilling life!

☐ No thanks, Sue. Fulfilling dreams with powerful mobility sounds too risky.

Checked Yes?
Let's rock n' roll!

Chapter One:
The Great American Mobility Gene

Americans hail from a wide variety of cultural backgrounds. As a result, many of us embrace hyphenated identities: German-American, Irish-American, Mexican-American, Taiwanese-American.

Yet there are two inheritances we all share in this land of the free and home of the brave.

The first is the American Dream, which we might define simply as the belief that human potential is endless.

The second significant inheritance is what I call the Great American Mobility Gene — the urge to move and groove as we fulfill our inalienable right to pursue freedom with gusto and pride. In the process, we define this nation and ourselves on our own terms.

Connect the American Dream with the Great American Mobility Gene and we have something incredibly powerful and purposeful. Witness:

- The Wright Brothers gave us wings.
- We won the Good War in the 1940s.
- We won the race to the moon.
- Our 20th Century auto industry provided post-war prosperity.
- We conquered tuberculosis and polio.
- Artists, musicians, writers, entrepreneurs, scientists, activists and athletes continue to express our nation's greatness in so many different ways that it is impossible to list them all here.

Despite these glorious achievements, throughout the last century we have developed a collective blind spot that borders on shameful.

Americans were born with the Great American Mobility Gene, but it is inevitable that our bodies age, transform, and may be afflicted with unforeseen physical setbacks and painful challenges. We often take for granted our speed, agility and the importance of our personal mobility. And we forget that losing mobility (i.e., our freedom and independence) can be profoundly harmful to our mental and emotional spirit.

I ask you, if we Americans have faced nearly every challenge imaginable and succeeded, why do we treat people who must live with a walker, wheelchair or cane - including our loved ones, including ourselves - as an afterthought? Why haven't we embraced this mobility challenge with the same fervor we call on when we defend our country or race to the moon?

Rather than create new independent living products that are technological marvels, Americans accept walkers, wheelchairs and canes in one drab, boring, unattractive color — gray, as well as the lazy and out-dated practice of attaching old tennis balls to the feet of walkers.

It is no wonder that lack of mobility harms self-esteem. We show little respect for people whose great American Mobility Gene has been altered. How would you feel living in a walker that screams "over the hill" or "damaged" or "less than whole"?

Mobility rehabilitation or Mobility Makeover is not nearly as challenging as finding a cure for cancer or inventing a long distance electric car. And statistics show that most Americans will require assisted mobility products of some kind at some point in their lives.

Yet despite coveting the status of being Number One in so many important categories, we choose to be second-rate...I venture to say last rate when it comes to Mobility Makeover consciousness.

Why, my fellow Americans? Why?

Chapter Two:
The D-Word Dictionary

Answers to tough questions about our collective health or American culture are hard to find. But as my Walker Stalker skills have evolved over eighteen years, I have come to believe that part of the problem is language: we love to label things.

So what's wrong with labels? Nothing if they are honest, positive, loving and even inspiring.

Unfortunately, as a people, we are prone to choose words that entrap and isolate rather than liberate the spirit.

That's why I've compiled the D-Word Dictionary. It includes only four words, but each defines a troubling aspect of our nature and reveals why I felt a need to stalk, to transform the industry and ultimately, to change the American mobility landscape.

- Discrimination.
- Denial.
- Depressing.
- Disability.

I've saved the worst for last. Americans use the word disability to describe those people who have a challenge that is thought to be different from a perceived "normal" state of being. The word is generously sprinkled in medical literature and well-intended government information and legislation.

For example, the Americans with Disabilities Act, approved in 1990, is an important milestone.

Title I of the Americans with Disabilities Act of 1990 prohibits private employers, state and local governments, employment agencies and labor unions from discriminating against qualified individuals with disabilities in job application procedures, hiring, firing, advancement, compensation, job training, and other terms, conditions, and privileges of employment. The ADA covers employers with 15 or more employees, including state and local governments. It also applies to employment agencies and to labor organizations. The ADA's nondiscrimination standards also apply to federal sector employees under section 501 of the Rehabilitation Act, as amended, and its implementing rules.

Even so, I believe it is an unfortunate name for a law that is meant to protect and empower. Personally, I find it difficult to use the word disability because it is so damning. Another D-Word. While I apologize for the profanity, labeling a person disabled is inaccurate and a curse that does not empower, enlighten or uplift.

Say the word out loud slowly and listen for the meaning. Dis-Ability. You mean, not able? Having no or limited ability?

This word is used freely in America to grossly and incorrectly define and describe 50 million people[1]. It has become a part of our culture. It has the power to destroy our inherent Great American Mobility Gene and our spirit.

---

1 *"United States Department of Labor: Office of Disability Employment Policy." FAQ: How many people with disabilities are there in the United States?. N.p., 2011. Web. 3 Oct 2011. <http://www.dol.gov/odep/faqs/people.htm>.*

The word Disability is like a wet, cold blanket. It lays a heavy burden on the shoulders of our nation. It also paves the way for other D-Word diseases.

Discrimination against those facing challenges.

Denial of the problem.

Depression among those whose mobility has been challenged, and among those who must care for a parent, child, friend or lover.

As the original Walker Stalker I have witnessed these problems first hand. So I am replacing the D-Word Dictionary with words that more accurately define American mobility.

- Empowered.
- Powerful.
- Independent.
- Uniquely able.
- Determined.
- Reinvention.
- Athlete.
- Beautiful.
- Proud.

The message is one that all human beings can embrace. It says that a change or transition in your Great American Mobility Gene does not negate your core essence.

You're still you!

You're still hot, sexy and smart!

You're also adventurous, opinionated, stylish, romantic and thoughtful!

You're even hopeful, ambitious, spunky, flirtatious...and so many other things that kindly and correctly define your endless physical, mental and spiritual potential!

I'm feeling better already...how about you?

Chapter Three:
Red Car, Red Toes
& Red Walker

My favorite part of Nova is our customers. I absolutely love connecting with them.

In the early days of Nova, circa 1994, we had a customer come by to get a tune up for her rolling walker. We had only sold a handful of this product at the time and meeting a Nova user was a huge treat. Her name was Yolanda. She was in her fifties and she was using a blue #4300 Explorer, the first in a long line of rolling walkers created by Nova. Yolanda spoke freely about her life and revealed that before she discovered the Explorer she was only able to walk a few steps at a time. Now that the Explorer was part of her life – and her personal mobility - she had worked up to walking a mile each day and doing so much. She was going to the park with her young grandchildren, making her famous chili for friends – and she confessed she also lost 30 pounds! Great, you might say, mission accomplished. The expanded mobility restored her independence.

Then something even better happened.

The rolling walker allowed Yolanda to be herself again. Her sweet, funny, sassy personality re-emerged, no longer masked by lack of mobility. At her core, Yolanda was a can-do kind of girl with just a hint of "bossy" thrown into the mix. The blue walker brought it out in her.

Getting to know this wonderful woman flipped a switch in me. It proved that mobility was not just a practical need. It was a form of personal expression. It was the logical outcome of being born with the

Great American Mobility Gene.

In the beginning, I was seeing solely the Nova product line and comparing it to my competition, searching for new ways to survive in a fiercely competitive market decided by insurance and Medicare allowables. After meeting Yolanda, I began to see people. Real people. Human beings. Many of them sharing similar challenges, but all unique in body, style and spirit.

Once human beings - my customers - became my focus, I looked at our products and something started bothering me. It irked me so much that I began to see red!

At the time, I drove a hot, red car. Every week I had a pedicure and had my toes painted red. It was a personal choice that made me feel sexy, alive and free.

Why didn't Yolanda, and others like her, have the same possibilities when they shopped for independent living products? Granted, at the time we did offer a blue walker. And even though in my opinion it was an ugly hue, it was still a radical step away from the institutional gray that dominated my industry.

Yet I was convinced that Yolanda would have chosen a hot red rolling walker if it had been available. Unfortunately, in 1994 nobody offered it. But that was about to change.

I was tired of serving the gray mobility monster. The Nova mission, my personal Walker Stalker mission, was to serve beautiful people like Yolanda and help them realize their potential while complimenting their personal and unique style. Nova was not only a business enterprise. It was an opportunity to connect and build human relationships that contributed to the American experience of excellence, liberty and freedom. Freedom to live. Freedom to dream.

Could we, would we create a sexy, hot red walker?

Heck yeah!

These were the guidelines for our new rolling walker:

- Make it a pretty red, just like the color I loved to see on my toes — rich and slightly lighter than garnet.
- Make it sleek —so that it traveled easily.
- Make it fun — name it Voyager and Cruiser Deluxe Walker, cool names that describe what it does.

America responded. Red became a hot seller. Red was spunky. Red was life-affirming. Red was independence.

Red opened the door to endless possibilities of personal expression for people whose precious mobility had been compromised.

Walker Stalker Confession:
Ride Sandy Ride...in Hot Red

I love getting letters from Nova customers. Over the years I have received many and I cherish them all. I'm moved that our customers would take the time to put pen to paper to share with me their Nova stories and Nova experiences.

These letters have been diverse, but they have all been meaningful to me. Some provide thoughtful and creative direction on how our products could be improved. Others are more direct, often including strongly-worded suggestions. Most of the letters express the sheer joy and jubilation that comes with mobility transformation.

About a year after we released the red Cruiser Deluxe walker, I received the most wonderful letter photo.

(Never hesitate to write a letter or email about a product or service. Companies that care, want to hear from you. Your feedback and inspiration could ignite a powerful new direction.)

Meet Sandy:

and

"Feb. 09, 1997

To Whom It May Concern:

I am so proud of my little candy apple red Nova Walker. It has saved my life and my sanity. I would like to tell you my story, and you can perhaps understand how much this walker means to me and the quality of life it has given back to me. I have had back problems for many years, but after working for aporximately ten years in a sales position I began having problems coping with the rigors of my job due to the continued deterioration of my back. I then went back to work for two more years in an office position where I could work at a desk. My back would no longer hold up to even this reduction in activity, and I was in such pain that I was reduced to laying flat on my back. I actually had to crawl on some bad days, as I could put weight on my back. I have always been an active person and I love to be with other people, and here I was flat on my back and going downhill physically as well as mentally. I was afraid if I stayed down too long I would never be able to get back up again. I kept trying to carry on as normal a life as I possibly could, but that proved impossible. I had seen your Nova walker in a medical supply company in my city, and I had spoken to a woman who bought one, and she said that she was very happy with hers. I told my husband that there was no longer any hope that I could navigate with assistance and he agreed to purchase one for me.

It is always hard to face the fact that you are disabled. We only give into our disabilities when there is

12

no other choice. I was at the point where I had no other choice. We picked out a candy apple colored Nova walker that matched our candy apple red Jeep that is our pride and joy. Being teenagers in the 1950's, we still loved to deck out a car with lots of chrome, etc. It is sharp looking and the walker fit in the back of the jeep perfectly.

I decided that I would not be embarassed by having to use a walker, and I decided to make it as much fun as I could. I still stand up as straight as I can, walk into any public place with a smile on my face and a thankful heart because I can be out and about again. I'm not saying I'm back to normal as I'm not, but I'm still trying to keep going as much as I can.

What has turned out to be so special is the attention that the Nova walker attracts. I went to an air show with my grandchildren and they got such a kick out of the fact that I couldn't get two feet without someone asking me about my walker. I went to Laughlin, Nevada, and I had to mail back information for some people in that area who were interested. I went to the Pomona Fair and the same thing happened. I went to Palm Springs and a couple stopped traffic on Palm Canyon Drive and wanted to know where they could buy one. As people were honking, I quickly gave them my phone number. They called me first thing the next morning and I gave them the address of the store where I purchased mine. I also loved mine so much I talked my mother-in-law into buying one. She has trouble breathing, and she can carry her oxygen in the basket and sit down when she is tired. I am almost always approached when I go out to eat or shop or whatever I do. I am so proud of my Nova walker and I'm always glad to share information with others. Even the younger people ask me how much I would charge to let them use my walker when they go to Disneyland. It is such a conversation piece that it has really become fun for me. It seems like everyone is interested in it. One thing that makes the walker so special is that the colors are bright and happy, it is well made, and it meets the needs of people like myself who have trouble walking and must sit down often.

So if you have to be disabled, at least you can do it in style...and I don't care how old we are, we still want to do things with style! As my husband says, "Always keep your cool!" I feel I'm still cool with my little red Nova walker. I really want to thank you for designing and selling such a great product and realizing people still enjoy nice, fun products even when struggling with life's challenges. The truth is that behind every sixty year-old face, there is still beats a sixteen year-old heart.

Sincerely,

Sandy Houghton"

Isn't Sandy the coolest!

Chapter Four:
Cane-Liosis: A National Epidemic

My Walker Stalker activities have uncovered many reasons for remaking the way we think and feel about independent living.

One of the most shocking was the discovery of an epidemic that has swept our nation and inflicted over 90 percent of people who use canes. I call it Cane-Liosis.

The name is probably new to you, but I bet you've already observed some of the more obvious symptoms:

- **Impaired mobility** – an uncertain struggle for each step
- **Improper body posture** – using the cane hunched over or too high with raised shoulders
- **Cane embarrassment** – you can see it on their face and in their body language...I hate my cane

It can be difficult watching someone suffering from Cane-Liosis. Hunched over or awkwardly struggling, it looks painful and humiliating. Many of us would prefer to look the other way. Yet the Walker Stalker knows that some day many of us may face these same mobility challenges.

So let's open our eyes, our minds and our hearts. We're all in this together. And, fortunately, Cane-Liosis is easily cured.

Just follow these quick and easy steps. (Or share them with someone you know could use a little help.)

The cane cure is easy to remember: Think shoes. Yes, hold in mind all of those glorious, beautiful and wonderful pairs of shoes that you need, want and love.

Step One: Size before you try

How to Fit a Cane

1. Wear your regular walking shoes.

2. The top of the cane should be even with the break in your wrist and/or your hip joint.

3. Place the cane 6" in front of you and 6" over to the side. Your elbow should be bent at a 20 to 30 degree angle.

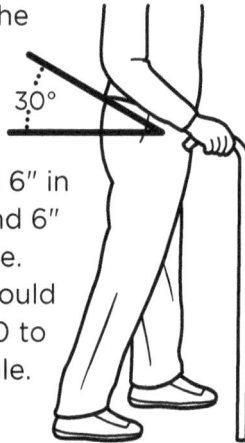

Most people walk with a cane that was never properly adjusted for their height. It's like wearing shoes that don't fit. It just doesn't feel right, it makes you unstable on your feet and it can cause physical pain and damage. When you shop for a pair of shoes, you are fitted for your correct size before you stand, walk and strut your stuff.

So, when shopping for a cane, think of it as a new pair of shoes. You want a style that makes you feel good about yourself and a size that is right for you. If something about your selection doesn't seem right, try another model.

In most cases, all you'll need is a simple

adjustment that matches the cane to your height. Once the measurement is right, your posture will improve, you'll feel upright, dignified and ready to face your day.

Makes sense, right? Yet, it is rarely done.

Step Two: Take care of your Treads and go Turbo!

The rubber tip on the bottom of your cane is your tread and therefore resembles the sole of a good shoe. It goes everywhere with you, indiscriminately taking all of the same steps and — like the sole of a shoe — the rubber tip helps to stop you from slipping. So a little maintenance is in order.

Check to see that the rubber tip on your cane is not worn down, worn through or uneven. This could cause imbalance and limit the motion and support of your cane. Tips are very easy to replace and they're really important — so don't skimp on your treads.

Want to take it up a notch? Turbo Tread your cane. A Turbo Tip with patented motion Tread Technology maximizes your natural walking stride and provides increased balance.

Turbo boost each step of your life!

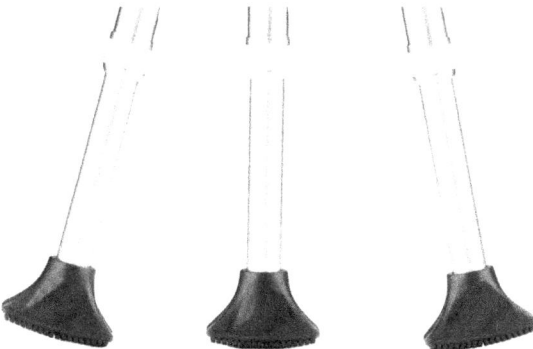

Guess what? The Turbo Tip costs about the same as a fancy coffee drink. Now that's a deal.

Step Three: Know when its time to move on

When your cane is old, used, worn and tired, it may just be time to get rid of that cane! After all, when you bought your first pair of adult shoes, did you expect to wear them the rest of your life?
Your cane is not only an important part of your mobility and physical health, it also contributes to your identity. If it is worn out and not truly serving you, don't wait — make a change. That doesn't mean you can't show some appreciation for all the steps your old cane has shared with you. By all means, praise it, honor it, and thank it for being a steady partner. But when it is time to retire old faithful, let it go.

Step Four: It's about style, baby!

Since your cane is a necessary part of you, it should be part of your daily personal style. Mix it up and match it up with your clothes and accessories; it deserves to be considered an element of your wardrobe, kind of like, you guessed it, a pair of shoes (and dare I say, a lot less expensive - you might consider getting more than one!).
Do you feel sexy, sophisticated, or edgy? Well, let your cane reflect who you truly are. Explore all of the cane colors and models that may compliment your many looks, seasonal trends and fashion choices. We are free to be ourselves, however that may change from day to day — even with independent living products. Have a Mobility Makeover by selecting a cane that is a personal expression, not just a pragmatic necessity. Be a Mobility Fashionista.

Walker Stalker Confession:
The Leopard Lady

Several years ago I attended a care-giver show and symposium outside of Chicago. I kept noticing a woman struggling with her old, gray cane; it looked like it was a hundred years old and had worn down tips. She seemed to take on the personality of her cane. Worn down and hunched over. I just had to stop her.

I asked her if anyone had ever adjusted her cane to her height and body. She looked at me so sweetly, but also with concern. She said, "Well...no...I've been using it like this for the past three years."

I thought, "That's over 1,000 days and probably millions of steps, all with the wrong sizing! Would anyone wear the wrong size shoes that long?"

She allowed me to adjust the handle of her cane to her wrist, which took all of a few seconds, and — bam! — after taking several trial steps with a cane that finally was properly adjusted, her entire face, spirit and body transformed.

She said, "I can't believe how much better I feel! My shoulder would ache with the cane raised up so high." Then she said to me with the biggest smile, "You're going to heaven for sure."

I thought, Me? The Walker Stalker? Wow, if that is all it takes, then I'm going to keep walking and stalking and spreading the word. The story does not end there...

The woman came around a few more times and I was so taken with her new stride and smile that I felt a crazy urge — yes, it was one of my Walker Stalker urges. My company had just come out with a new leopard-print cane. Hmm. Should I do it? Snap decision: I'm going for it.

I stopped this lovely lady once more and asked if she would mind if I traded in her old, worn down gray cane for a new leopard-print cane. She went wild — literally. She was ecstatic and started telling me all about her personal style and the long forgotten but coveted pieces of clothing she has in leopard print. "I'm bringing back my leopard style. Can't wait for bridge with the ladies tomorrow! I'm going to wear my hot leopard blouse with my new leopard cane!"

My new friend gave me the biggest hug. I proudly confess that she was now walking well and with a strut and shake in her powerful stride. That's right, sister! Walk the walk in all of your hotness! She had something special in her all along. It was the old, ugly cane that had caused the dreaded Cane-Liosis and made her forget her inner strength and natural feline style.

Life is too beautiful — you are too beautiful — we all are too beautiful — to walk with an ugly, old, worn down cane.

Chapter Five:
Lose the Tennis Balls

Lose the Tennis Balls
Unsafe   Unsanitary   Unattractive

Get Walker Skis   nova
www.NovaMedicalProducts.com

Tennis balls cut open and stuck on the bottom of walkers is a ubiquitous image in any senior center or assisted care facility. The practice of using recreational balls on the back two legs of a walker was even a sight-gag in the Oscar-nominated animated film, *Up*.

But do tennis balls really belong on walkers? Absolutely not!

Then why do walker stalkers see the yellow or lime colored eyesores so often? I have asked many people this question, including doctors, physical therapists, caregivers, the product users, and even PhD gerontologists.

In all cases, I get two answers:

1. "That's what I have always seen, so I thought that was what you were supposed to do."

2. "I have no idea."

I've got nothing against tennis balls. In fact, I love them. Tennis is one of my favorite sports to play and watch, and it's a great feeling to whack the heck out of a fresh, new tennis ball.

I also love dogs and their obsession with fetching anything that is tossed near or far, and the tennis ball just happens to be perfect for this activity.

But would I slice open tennis balls and fit them on the bottom of a baby stroller or skateboard? Of course not. That would be crazy. Would I stick them on the bottom of my favorite high heels and walk around town? Are you out of your mind???

It is equally wrong to apply fuzzy, rubber orbs on the feet of walkers.

Why? Let me count the ways.

They are unsafe: They accelerate wear and tear while actually making the walker unstable. They can rip and wear down easily catching on surface bumps, blips and imperfections. Often, they are completely worn through and the user doesn't even know it – exposing the metal shaft to scrape along – damaging both the walker and the floors.

They are unsanitary: The fabric collects and then tracks germs anywhere and everywhere the user goes...bathroom to kitchen to bedroom...yuck!

They are unattractive: They are a disrespectful "embellishment" that stigmatizes the millions of people who rely on walkers for their mobility. I'm 100% sure no one has ever said or thought, "I just love these dirty old tennis balls on my gray old walker. That really is so me!"

People use tennis balls because they believe it will help the walker glide more smoothly over various types of floors and terrains. Not so. Meanwhile, there are many walker glide products available that will do the trick. Fortunately, NOVA has created a product that we hope will make tennis balls a thing of the past, except for tennis players and dogs, of course. We call them - Walker Skis.

These sporty accessories look like very short skis, and can easily be installed on the legs of most walkers.   They are durable, stylish, easy-to-clean, and unlike tennis balls, they are made specifically to improve the mobility of walkers.

Every time I see someone using a walker with tennis balls I cringe. I know that they are in jeopardy. I also cringe when I see my competitors make and sell walker attachments that actually hold the tennis balls. Really? That's the best you can do?? Are you serving our customer???

I also know that people facing mobility challenges still want to be stylish (remember the leopard lady?) and dignified — and why not? Would anyone in their right mind stick tennis balls on the heels of their Manolos, Christian Louboutins, or favorite cowboy boots? Americans deserve better. (And I do mean Americans; I've never seen tennis balls on walkers outside of the U.S. – not something that should fill us with national pride.)

Walker Stalker Confession:
The Lily of Hermosa Beach

Wow, I have so much to confess here. I just can't help myself when it comes to tennis balls or some crazy non-glide contraption on walkers.

I've stopped people in the airport, at Los Angeles Philharmonic performances at the Walt Disney Concert Hall, my dentist's office, hotels, streets, and on promenades. I've even videotaped someone while driving in my car. (It's not something I'm proud to admit, but I'm being honest here!) Here's how it happened.

I was driving along Pacific Coast Highway in Hermosa Beach and the traffic was so slow I couldn't help notice a woman on the sidewalk. She was moving with the aid of an old folding walker. It was bad enough that she had tied grocery bags to the sides of the flimsy walker. Worse — get this! — wooden blocks were wedged onto the back feet of the walker. Wooden blocks?   I couldn't believe what I was seeing. No wonder she was moving very cautiously and at a rate that was, at best, glacial.

I took out my camera and started filming video of her. Confession: I was still driving at the time, albeit very slowly, but I don't recommend doing this. Not ever. It's possible to take walker stalker behavior too far, and that day, I did. Later, I watched the video many times trying to understand why — why some human beings had to suffer this way? Then fate came into play.

I was at an art festival in Hermosa Beach when my friend Shauna nudged me. I had told her all about the lady with the wooden blocks. Now I heard her say, "Sue, there she is! There's the lady with the wooden blocks on her walker!"

When I approached her, the woman told me her name was Lily. I'm sure she was a little concerned being approached by a complete stranger who had videotaped her on the street and was now insisting that she come in to my office so I could give her a mobility makeover. (No, I did not introduce myself as The Walker Stalker!) But I couldn't blame her for wondering, who the heck is this lady insisting that I need new equipment? Lily remained a bit skeptical. So I gave her my business card and begged her to call me.

Two weeks passed and I heard nothing. Finally, Lily's great granddaughter, Ariana called. I explained who I was and assured her that I only wanted to help. She convinced Lily that they should accept my offer and we agreed to meet at Nova.

On the day of their visit, I learned that Lily was a social butterfly and practically the mayor of Hermosa Beach. Every day she would go out and about to local spots like The Mermaid restaurant to call on friends, or to run errands and help others, or simply to put a smile on someone's face.

Lily was 93 years young — vibrant and lovely — and lived by herself. Her old gray walker with wooden blocks was an insane match for such a beautiful physical being and spectacular spirit. It was like forcing Michael Jordan or Kobe Bryant to wear worn down flip flops during a basketball game. Or making the Queen mum carry a brown paper bag as her purse.

For Lily, we did a double mobility makeover with one walker for outside use and one walker for inside use. For inside use, she chose a pretty pink folding walker with a front bar floral design, walker skis, of course, cup holder and black walker bag. For her outside walker, Lily chose a red GetGO Classic in red because it matched her nails and accessorized it with a cup holder, flashlight and butterfly saddle bag.

Guess what was the first thing Lily did when she took her new walkers for a test drive? She grooved her body – doing a shake and a shimmy. Grooving your body is the natural thing to do when you are excited about life. Movin' and Groovin' – it just feels good. So, of course I would have to name our next rolling walker – The GetGO Groove – inspired by Lily's amazing groove for life.

There are millions of amazing people like Lily who deserve better. Who among us would willingly clip the wings of such a lovely social butterfly? It's not right that society is apparently blind to the demeaning nature of drab, dilapidated mobility equipment.

We have the responsibility to know better and do better.

I say, LOSE THE TENNIS BALLS and get some Walker Skis. It's time to glide to a better independent living future.

One of Nova's missions is to Lose the Tennis Balls on all walkers in America. We're going to do it! One person at a time, one assisted living residence at a time, one city at a time...until the entire country is walker-tennis ball free.

Chapter Six:
Mobility Makeover:
Expressing the Icon that is You

My aunt Angela is one of my great role models. At age 40, she left her life in Taiwan and moved to David, Florida to help my family after my father passed away. She was always willing to sacrifice for others.

My aunt was also a woman of great style. It was through her that I first heard the name Yves Saint Laurent. She was proud of her special YSL designer accessories — scarves, sunglasses, gloves — that reflected her strong sense of self and personal panache.

Her influence on me was profound. She inspired me to develop my own tastes and love for things like dazzling peep-toe pumps and strappy 4" heels or a must-have handbag.

But Yves Saint Laurent, a true icon of fashion, also became a guiding light. And so I would turn to him when I was searching for inspiration. Before long, I discovered a short and simple quote — only five words — yet powerful too.

"Fashions Fade, Style is Eternal."

I loved those words immediately, but it took me longer to truly understand and appreciate what he was saying.

Fashions FADE, Style is ETERNAL

We age every day. If that troubles you, look at it this way: it takes each and every one of those days and all the years from youth to maturity to make us more beautiful. Personal style and true beauty is created over long stretches of time, not over night.

In other words, to age is to become who we truly are. Fashions will come and go, but our own individual, soulful sense of style evolves and endures over time.

Yet we don't always trust this special, inherent quality; especially when hardship suddenly restricts mobility. I've learned that many good people with unique gifts suddenly forsake their flair and grudgingly join an army of conformity — the users of gray, drab hospital gear – when their mobility is challenged.

Why? It takes years, in most cases, to truly come into our own. Why give up on it? The world needs that "thing", that joie de vivre, that makes us each an icon, individual and unique.

You say you're not an icon? I disagree. YOU ARE. Your history, your challenges, your triumphs, your imprint all distinguish you from others. Hello individuality, goodbye generality.

To assist your transformation, Nova has coined some new fashion terms. Grandma Chic replaces "old lady." And Grandpa Cool trumps "old man." Facing mobility challenges at a younger age? Choose your moniker: Mobility Fashionista. Holy Roller. Yes I Cane. Walk 'n' Roller. Movin' Groover. (I could go on and on...)

Name it and claim it because we've got work to do, people to see and places to go.

You have lived — you're still living, passionately, courageously — and I need your help to change the way the world looks at you. It won't be easy. But I have a plan: Let your eternal style shine through.

Think style is shallow? Not so. Your personal style may be expressed externally, but its origin is deep within you. I could see it in the eyes of the

Leopard Lady and Lily of Hermosa Beach. I could hear it in their voices and choice of words. I read it in Sally's letter too. What speaks is actually spirit and soul, an expression of the love you have for this singular life. It is born of all that you've seen and experienced. It is timeless and memorable.

Fashions Fade, Style is Eternal

When physical changes create limitations, they may temporarily mask the icon that is you. Since you are the choices you make, it is Nova's mission to provide you with options to make the best possible choices to reflect your spirit and style with beautiful and exciting independent living products that —

- Empower
- Improve
- Dignify
- Express
- Magnify your inner you

mobility
makeover

The Mobility Makeover is about rediscovering, transforming and empowering what is the most important part of your life — your mobility. The transformation begins with three easy steps:

1. Maximize your Mobility

- Let's get you moving and grooving better, faster, and safer. Maximize your mobility by choosing a new Rolling Walker, a designer cane, or simply replacing those tennis balls with Walker Skis. Let's get you back in the joy of life, interacting with friends, family and community.

2. Maximize your Function

- Let's get you doing more, sharing more and allowing you to be more of who you truly are — in action and ability. We achieve this by having great functioning mobility options. Think of a Rolling Walker as your new set of wheels. If you bought a new automobile, wouldn't you accessorize it to make the ride more pleasurable? You bet. That's why Nova has created lightweight walker attachments, such as cup holders and gourmet food trays. Flashlight and travel bag add-ons can also maximize your function so that you maximize you!

3. Maximize your Style

- You've had personal style your entire life; no need to invent it. What we're creating is a new awareness of it and options to reflect it — a reminder — so that you keep it present and powerful. Your cane, walker, or transport chair is now a part of you and your personal style. Customize it with colors and accessories that truly reflect who you are. Nova's extensive line of mobility fashion bags, for example, will add hot style and fabulous function to your mobility. And, don't forget to mix it up with your style whims, mood, newest trends and seasonal inspiration.

The Ultimate
Mobility Makeover

The Ultimate Mobility Makeover will go way beyond you to include all those important people around you — friends, family, co-workers — beyond to your community, your state, the rest of America and, some day, the world. You will inspire them with your special brand of MAS appeal — Mobility, Ability and Style. You will change the landscape of consciousness with every step you take following your Mobility Makeover.

America needs you to share your story, share your strength and share your iconic mission. Help the people around you dump those awful, frumpy "D" words:

- Denial
- Depressing
- Discrimination
- Disability

Hey, style icon, show the world how unique you are!

Walker Stalker Confession:
Bad Ass meets Lady Love

I like to go on Nova mission field trips. My favorite destinations are assisted-living communities and resorts. You may have an image in your head of a hospital-type home or a sad final destination.

Get that out of your mind. Think college days. Many of these communities are full of fun, socializing, unbridled joy and adventure. After all, life is meant to be fulfilling at all ages, not just in our youth. And that's the message being shared across America at the many locales I visit each year.

Not long ago, I went to an assisted living facility in Henderson, Nevada to do a Mobility Makeover presentation. I was so pleased when many residents showed up with their cool walkers and stylish canes.

One gentleman sat right up front and quickly let me know that he was saving the seat next to him. He was handsome, charming and a bad ass (my favorite combination). The leg he lost during World War II had been replaced with a prosthetic limb.

About 15 minutes into my presentation, a lovely lady appeared and sat down in the seat my war veteran had been saving. As I continued my presentation, I could not help but notice how the two related: obviously flirtatious, sexy looks back and forth, comments and nudges.

After my presentation I had to ask, "Is there something going on between the two of you?"

The lovely lady responded very coolly. "Well, I did just wake up from a nap...in his room." (as she patted down her slightly ruffled hair)

When I looked at the handsome, charming bad ass for confirmation, he winked at me.

Yes, indeed. Regardless of age, you can still heat it up.

You Can Still Heat It Up!   *Cocktails: a must, Bathing suit: optional.*

Chapter Seven:
Your New Set of Wheels

Getting a new set of wheels has been something we have looked forward to since we were kids. Would there be a new, shiny red bike under the Christmas tree? Waiting outside with a bow on it one birthday morning? Then when we did finally get that new bike, we just couldn't wait to explore, go, do, and see. Ahhh, the joy and freedom that new bike gave us.

Next we upgrade our hopes to a set of wheels that is an American rite of passage. Maybe you started with the old family station wagon or your older brother's beat up Mustang. Doesn't matter the vintage or history — you had wheels to explore, go, do and see. Ahhh, the joy and freedom that first car gave us. It doesn't stop there. Next in line is the set of wheels you always dreamed of having. The hot red sports car, the all-terrain four-wheel drive, the super fuel efficient green car, or the sleek sedan with all of the best features and bling. Ahhh, the joy and freedom that dream car gave us.

When it's time to choose yet another new set of wheels, remember that mobility is an essential part of that spirit that wants to explore, go, do and see.

Your new set of wheels — your new rolling walker — should be what you want, should allow you to do want you want, and it should look the way you want it to look. After all, from the time you were a kid, you looked forward to your mobility and what it would bring to your life — new adventures, new freedoms.

Hold onto that excitement. Be decisive and discerning when choosing your new set of wheels.

Six S's for Choosing your Rolling Walker

When we shop for a car — especially a dream car — we usually have a list of factors we must satisfy before actually making a purchase. The same should be true when you're in the hunt for your ideal walker. The Six S guidelines will help you compare features and benefits.

1. Safety

- Your safety is the most important part of your mobility. So work with a trained and knowledgeable medical professional when choosing the right independent living product for you.

- I also recommended that you consult with your doctor about any mobility products you are using or considering for purchase. Read and understand all guide books, cautions and warnings that accompany each product. Do this before you take your new set of wheels for a spin. If you are unsure of what to choose, call a member of your support team — your doctor, the medical equipment department specialist or a Nova customer service associate.

- For example, you should know that when using a rolling walker, the seat is for stationary seating only. The walker is not a go-cart.

2. Sizing

- Every person is unique in size, shape, ability and personal preferences. So it is important that your mobility products are properly selected to fulfill your particular needs.

- Always provide your accurate height and weight so that each product can be properly adjusted for you. This is important, because you want the product to live up to its overall safety and performance standards, as well as feel good with your body.

- It is also important to provide your Home Health specialist information about your current physical condition and history with mobility products. Communicating how you feel is always important. But in this case it will allow your Home Health specialist to assist you in making adjustments to the walker you choose.

3. Stability
- With your new set of wheels, you need to have stability and control. That's why the hand brakes on your rolling walker are so important. They allow you to control your speed, which is the key to your stability.

- The hand brakes are similar to the ones we all have used on a bicycle. To control the speed, rest your palm on the hand grip and use your fingers to pull up on the brake lever. Nova's brakes are uniquely designed for optimum control, and they are well suited for all hand sizes. They work particularly well for small, weak or arthritic hands with the distance to engage the brake about 1 inch. How's that for control! You don't want your hand brake to be an exercise causing strain and fatigue to your hands.

- To lock the hand brakes, push down on the brake lever all the way to the stop or click. Be sure the hand brakes are in the locked or parked position when seated. The locked position is also a great way to improve stability when standing in place. To release the locked brakes, pull up on the lever. And, because we know how cool our customers are, we added reflectors on the back of our hand brakes.

4. Seat

- Having a nice, comfy seat on your rolling walker is convenient and very cool. Now, you don't have to worry about getting tired on a walk or finding a place to sit and rest. Your very own front-row seat to the spectacle of life is with you at every turn. You can choose from a firm plastic or padded seat. You can even add a custom snow leopard seat cover! Remember, it's all about you and your iconic style.

5. Storage

- Your ride is also about your personal stuff and all of the things you need to strut, stroll and strive. Rolling walkers come with storage options to carry all kinds of items. You can choose from a front removable basket or a secure under-seat pouch. You can even add to or customize those storage options with basket liners, additional mobility bags and even a trendy camouflage print cell phone bag.

- This S, storage also means storing your rolling walker and taking it where you want. You can easily fold up the rolling walker and away we go!

- The most common request I have received from Nova customers over the years was to develop a way to lock and unlock the walker in the folded position so it would be easier to lift and carry.

Well...we've done it! Our latest patent pending innovation is called the Lock n' Load and this feature will come standard on all Nova rolling walkers beginning in Fall 2011.

6. Style

- Did you love your bike because it was cool blue, or your mustang because it was hot red? Everyone has a mobility style that expresses who they really are. What's your pick for your new set of wheels? Pink, red, black or purple? How about a trendy green or sophisticated blue? And the super stylish bags and seat/back covers? Take it to the limit! Yes! Bling your ride with the color and accessories that say, Watch out, here I come! And watch those heads turn. That's right! People love to check out what is cool, what is hot, and what is amazing.

How do you roll?
Ride-in-Style
Transport Chairs & Wheelchairs

Here's the blunt truth: no one wants to be in a wheelchair or transport chair. No one. When we see someone in a wheelchair, we all hope that will not be our fate.

But if that does happen, and your body must adapt to a new mode of movement — your mobility is still yours. Why? Because your life is still yours and the world is still yours.

One of my first Nova independent reps was a great guy named John. He was paraplegic. Other than my childhood friend Jason Shomer who had muscular dystrophy, I had never spent much time with someone in a wheelchair. John showed me the daily details of living with his set of wheels and how normal and abnormal life becomes.

- Working with John — normal.
- Making sales calls with John — normal.

Well, normal is not the right word because John was such a great sales rep. Better than most. And, he was nicer than most. He would always open the door, insist on carrying the equipment, and do the heavy lifting.

The only part of being with John that was abnormal was the so-called normal world around us. There was a lot of uncertainty, for example, when getting seated at a restaurant or boarding an airplane. There was also disappointing human behavior when the handicapped parking spot was illegally taken or blocked. Or when there were no support bars in a restaurant bathroom. And I discovered that wheelchair ramps were a glaring rarity.

There is so much to know and understand about wheelchairs. I highly recommend that you consult a rehab/wheelchair professional — especially if the wheelchair is for more than occasional or light use. (The recommendations included here are mostly for occasional or light use of a wheelchair or transport chair.)

A Basic Transport Chair & Wheelchair Q & A

Frequently asked questions deserve clear answers. If you need more information than I provide here, please call on your doctor, a sales person or a Nova customer service associate.

Q: What's the main difference between a Wheelchair and a Transport Chair?

A: Wheelchairs with large 24" rear wheels/rims can be self-propelled by the user or pushed by the companion. This feature adds more weight and bulk to the wheelchair.

Transport chairs have smaller rear wheels, with 8" or 12" diameters. As a result, the user cannot self propel and must be pushed by a companion or courtesy staff member at a concert hall, for example. Thus, the transport chair is both lighter and more compact than the wheelchair. This can be incredibly helpful to the companion or care-giver who must lift the chair when storing in a car.

Q: The Brakes — Who's in Control? (Option for Transport Chairs)

A: Some transport chairs come with both rear-wheel locks and locking hand brakes on the handles controlled by the person pushing the chair. This allows the care-giver or ride provider to control both the speed of the ride and then safely park the chair by locking the brakes. This is a great option and promotes safety for those bumpy or hilly terrains. Make sure to fasten your seat belt!

Weight and Width Matter

Be sure to match the weight capacity and the seat width of the transport chair or wheelchair to the user. You should also carefully consider the actual weight of the wheelchair or transport chair, especially if there are many events and adventures in your mobility makeover plan.

Ride in Style

Choose the color and options that complement your own personal style and life-style. Add a leopard Mobility Clutch for your cell phone, a flashlight attachment for the evening stroll, or Butterfly Saddle Bags for your personal belongings.

Walker Stalker Confession:
Connoisseur of Life

When you least expect it, an angel will come into your life and you will be blessed. Denise is that angel for me. I thought that I had a pretty good grasp on my industry and I was on a mission to transform our way of seeing and implementing mobility. I was, after all, the walker stalker and mobility makeover maven.

Well, the truth is, I still have much to learn and experience. I had never fully lived with my product or loved with my product. Denise changed that.

I met Denise in late 2010. She came to the Nova office to get a tune up to the brakes on her rolling walker. Some of my staff had already met her and told me about this beautiful and amazing lady who was a huge Nova walker fan.

When I heard she was at the office, I ran out to meet her and her mother Selma. We connected instantly. Denise has the most sparkling blue eyes I have ever seen and they express her vibrant and glowing spirit. We chatted a bit, then I asked her if I could interview her so that Nova could share with others her wisdom, experience and insights about living with ALS, also known as Lou Gehrig's Disease, or in my opinion — the cruelest disease.

As I listened to Denise talk about her Nova walker, her mobility inventions (like making her own water bottle holder), going on a walking tour of Paris, photographing the emperor penguins in Antarctica, and living life to the fullest despite ALS, I found myself completely raw with emotion and I had to hold back my tears. I was honored that she chose Nova as a partner in her amazing life. She is a Nova hero.

As Nova CEO, I can talk a great deal about mobility and independence. But when Denise talks about these topics, she is talking about her reality.   It is the way she lives her life, each and every day. And Denise loves life. She loves life more than anyone I have ever met. She's an explorer, a photographer, a truth speaker. She's a life connoisseur.

Denise and I have become dear friends and she invited me to visit and stay with her at her lovely home in Palm Springs. Well, I have never been to a home more beautifully expressed. The care that went into every choice can best be described as the Ritz Carlton with a motherly embrace.

We had a blast! We cruised all over a local

and massive art fair purchasing so many wonderful things that we looked like shopping divas, with so many shopping bags, by the end of the day. We did so much, but my favorite part of the weekend was lounging on her couch at the end of the night as we had the best girl talk about life, relationships, ALS, fears, hopes, dreams, and even dying.

Denise truly is a connoisseur of life. She can see, hear, taste, know and appreciate how incredibly beautiful life is, and she is a reflection of life's beauty. ALS has robbed Denise of her mobility and muscular function, but her heart, mind and spirit explode with a vitality that the rest of us can only envy.

I learned something so important during my weekend with Denise. I wanted to help her with simple chores around the house — walking over to close the blinds, picking up after myself, – but Denise didn't need that at all. Through smart planning, strategic practice, innovative procedures and amazing efficiency, Denise was more than able to take care of herself. She could have and wanted to take care of me. That's right — take care of me. She expressed such joy, genuine joy in doing things for me. It's such a universal sentiment, to want to be needed by and give to others. It makes us feel good about ourselves. And just because someone is facing a mobility challenge doesn't mean that they don't get that same joy from giving to others. When I finally realized that this was Denise's wish, I basked in the love of being taken care of by an Angel.

Sue and Denise

Stormin' Norman: 92 going on 50

You know what? It turns out that Denise is a walker stalker too! Shhhhh....

Proud of her Nova walker and independence, for months Denise had been suggesting to her dear friend Norm that he too use a walker.   At 92, Norm was experiencing some mobility challenges, but he had defiantly refused any help and insisted that he would never use a walker — never!

Even so, with her electric blue eyes, the beautiful Denise can be very persuasive. She eventually enticed Norm to accept my gift of a Mobility Makeover.

Denise was thrilled. But she called to warn me that Norm would be tough to convert. I was ready for the challenge.

Norm arrived with quite an entourage — Denise, her mother Selma (one of Norm's dearest friends) and a very lovely, young lady. I wondered who this lady might be. In my limit creating brain, I assumed she must be Norm's caregiver. Good thing I kept my mouth shut.

This gorgeous lady was Norm's smokin' hot wife and the room sizzled when they glanced at each other.

I truly enjoy the Mobility Makeovers because the first step is to get to know the person. I soon learned that Norm is quite a man. He was a World War II veteran and photographer, a successful entrepreneur, toy king, world traveler, amazing golfer, motor home navigator extraordinaire. He was 92 going on 50!

Norman really opened up when I explained that selecting a rolling walker was not a surrender but an expression of his life and all the wonderful opportunities that lay ahead. He shared with me how he missed walking his beloved golf course.

"Don't view your walker as a symbol of what you can't do, but what you can and want to do. Let it define your life in a positive way." Then I laid out all the options — colors, sizes, wheels, accessories — and let Norman choose his new set of wheels.

That weekend he golfed again, went for long walks with his wife Gilyn - with his new mobility partner.

Norm is now a passionate walker advocate. And he insists that all his converts splurge and treat themselves to all the cool stuff and mobility gadgets! Why not? Express yourself!

Norm is an American Hero and my hero. He found love again at 90, smiles with the kind of charm and charisma that makes you giddy, and walks forward in life with a stride that is the epitome of the Great American Mobility Gene.

From Left to Right: Me, Denise, Norman, & Gilyn

Secret Bonus Chapter 7.5:
Where to begin: Be Cool, Be Kind, Just Ask and Make Eye Contact

Want to experience the joy of becoming a walker stalker? It's simple. Start by listening. When you begin your Walker Stalker activities, you may think you know exactly what kind of Mobility Makeover is needed. But be careful how you approach your new friends. Sometimes over-confidence comes off as arrogant and may suggest an insecure need to lecture. Don't be a know it all.

Instead, begin by getting past the physical person by making eye contact. Looking into someone's eyes allows you to see the real person and the real unique spirit that is often over-shadowed by the exterior physical being. Next, instead of assuming, insisting, or ignoring, just ask.

When I met the Leopard Lady I merely inquired if she would allow me to adjust her cane. I didn't insist. When you ask instead of tell, it shows confidence and humility. It expresses your interest in having a human exchange that is secure, strong and kind.

If you don't know what to do or what to say in an uncomfortable situation, just ask a question with a kind heart and thoughtful mind, from one human being to another:

- "May I help you?"
- "May I ask what happened?"
- "What can I do to make this work?"
- "How would you like me to help?"

You can even ask permission to ask. Just don't be afraid to ask.

Also, remember that a physical difference doesn't make a person less than human, incomplete or incapable. I have witnessed many well-intentioned people make the same mistake: They speak as if the person using a wheelchair or walker lacks mental or emotional capabilities, when in fact all they have is a physical challenge. Again, look past the physical and into a person's eyes. That will help you connect and communicate with the real person because you're not talking to the wheelchair or walker.

We are all equal, we all have a mind, and we all have a soul. Don't assume, don't ask around someone, don't ignore.

But DO ask. It's human to be curious. It's human to care. And remember the powerful and universal message that I'm sure you already know:

Do unto others, as you would have them do unto you.

Chapter Eight:
The Secret Weapon:
A Unique & Powerful Bond

The unique bond between grandchildren and grandparents is one of the most beautiful, pure, and powerful relationships that exist. They have a deep love and influence over each other that shapes our lives and fills our hearts.

I was fortunate to have all four grandparents alive during my formative years. They were Grandma and Grandpa Lee and Grandma and Grandpa Chen. Grandma Lee passed away in 2002, Grandpa Chen in 2008 and Grandma Chen in 2009. Grandpa Lee is doing very well at 96 and is a proud Nova walker user and a seasoned walker stalker. All four of these completely unique individuals contributed to my DNA and spirit, and have therefore influenced my past, present and, no doubt, my future.

Grandparents do so much for us. They embrace us with incredible warmth and joy. They look at us with adoring eyes that express unconditional love, excitement and enthusiasm. They tell us stories that make our imaginations soar. They influence us and we influence them, often in ways more subtle than our parents. They also defend us as though it was a Supreme Court case, and brag about us as though we have won the Nobel Peace Prize.

It's often different from a parent/child relationship, softer and more accepting. And it's also why a grandparent's mobility has a direct impact on the whole family. Grandparents and grandchildren want to be able to spend active time together, and mobility equipment is often the catalyst for making that possible.

The fact that I only know how to courteously speak my native language of Taiwanese is a testament to my grandmothers, although there are some curious drawbacks. Since my grandmothers only said the nicest things to me, I struggle a bit with my native tongue when trying to express some not-so-nice things. Can you believe that I don't know a single "bad" word in Taiwanese? Even my anger is polite! My grandmothers were lovely ladies.

Grandpa Chen had a tough skin and could be imperious. No one had ever told him what to do. It was always his way or his way. My father and uncles would never challenge or question him — ever. Day to day, this could be arduous to those closest to him, but I give this great man tremendous credit for his vision and incredible determination.

In Nova's early years I was experiencing paint problems on our rolling walkers. They would arrive with minor scratches. Not acceptable to my customers or to me. I raised this issue with Grandpa Chen and he immediately and passionately wanted to fix the glaring, though admittedly slight, imperfections. So we paid a visit to the paint factory. What we encountered was a horrible, awful place. The fumes, the reckless disposal of toxic waste, the inhuman labor conditions ...

I did not have to say a word. Grandfather decided right then that he would build his own paint factory. It would be a state-of-the-art facility, a marvel of engineering that exceeded all environmental regulations. Once the new plant was ready, Grandpa Chen pledged that he would paint the Nova walkers so that each one was as perfect as the surface of a shiny new car.

Grandpa's paint factory was built in record time and, as promised, set exceptional standards for cleanliness and efficiency. To this day, our walkers have a paint finish that stands alone in our industry. The walkers shine as they should — like their owners.

This was just one of the many factory buildings that my grandfather would envision and then build with that determined and sometimes scary, crazy will of his.

One thing I learned from him: sometimes crazy is good. Try to sell a red walker when all that was out there was gray? Crazy! But we did it, and it worked.

In 2000, an earthquake in our city of Taichung destroyed over 700 buildings; and more than 2,700 lives were lost. All factories were shut down — some for days, most for months.

Yet Grandpa Chen's factories and buildings did not have a single crack. They were up and running within a day, a testament to the superior engineering and Grandpa Chen's determination.

So how did this formidable man treat his grandchildren?

He softened when spending time with us. He even accepted my amazing sister Tina (a talented physical therapist with my father's gift for healing and inspiring her patients) occasionally bossing him around. When Tina would find him to be grossly out of line, she wouldn't stand for it.

And Tina had a strong influence over him. She warmed his hardened heart by constantly hugging him and even washing his broken down feet. She spoke to him from such a deep, loving place that this tough guy — our grandfather the master builder — began to feel love, hurt, humility, generosity and compassion in new ways.

My uncles called this change a miracle; something they never would have thought could happen to their father.

At the 20-year anniversary party of Nova

Taiwan, I went on stage to attempt a speech in my native Taiwanese. With my very limited Taiwanese vocabulary, I thanked my grandfather for having the faith in me to start Nova USA, when I was just 23. When I finished and returned to my table, Ron, my partner told me. "I don't know what you said, but your grandfather is over there crying."

No one had ever seen Grandpa Chen shed tears. This is how I know that the connection between a grandparent and grandchild has no rival. The love is a gift that has the potential to transform. It is a secret weapon against conformity, stubbornness and the wide-spread hospital-gear mentality that we must change.

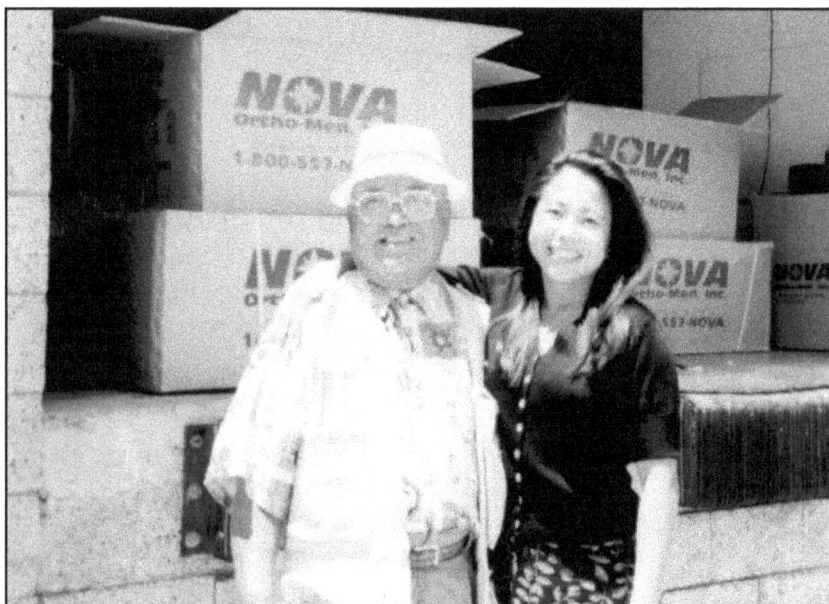

Grandpa Chen & me - 1995

Tapping into this wonderful bond can affect a Mobility Makeover by encouraging a grandparent that embracing their mobility equipment means more meaningful time together.

A couple of years ago during a visit to a large assisted-living center, I enjoyed a rare sighting of a man who used a purple Nova Cruiser Deluxe Walker. Purple is one of my all-time favorite colors. One reason I love it so much is because I consider it a tribute to the Los Angeles Lakers who won a 3-Peat NBA Championship, from 2000-2002. (Yes, this Walker Stalker is also a basketball fanatic.)

As much as I love the color, I knew it was never going to sell in numbers that challenged red or blue — the preferred colors at the center I was visiting. That's why it surprised me to see this guy with a swagger in his step rolling with purple! He had chosen some cool accessories, too, like the food tray and mobility bag.

I had to meet him, so I asked where he got his walker. His answer was as confident and "cocky" as his stride. It was also a revelation.

"Well, my granddaughter came to visit me and she got on the in-ter-net and wanted me to have a very special walker — different from everyone here — and she picked out this fabulous purple walker just for me. Isn't that great! Don't you just love my walker!"

Yes, I loved his walker. But what I loved even more was that his granddaughter had picked it out for him because he deserved something special.

I'm quite certain that this young woman knew intuitively that a purple walker would put the swagger back in her grandfather's step. He was transformed simply by trading in his standard gray bent-metal walker for the hottest walker in the world — his world.

The pride he expressed was, for me, the most moving part of the experience. The man beamed. He was so proud that his granddaughter cared enough about him to participate in his mobility makeover and provide a new set of purple wheels.

Walker Stalker Confession:
Grandpa Mission Accomplished

Once I had discovered the secret weapon, grandchildren, I decided to test the idea in the field. An independent pharmacy show in Altoona, Pennsylvania was the perfect occasion.

While sharing information at the NOVA booth, a family walked by and I could not help overhear an exchange between the husband and wife.

"Dad really needs one of those fancy walkers, but he refuses to use one. He said he would rather fall than use a walker."

I had to know more. The Walker Stalker strikes again!

When I stopped the couple to inquire about their situation, they told me about the horrible resistance and battles that resulted from trying to convince their father to use a walker. It can put a strain on a parent-child relationship when the roles are reversed – even if by necessity. The child — now an adult that is trying to act responsibly — is calling the shots for a parent who needs help but finds it difficult to relinquish control.

I noticed the couple had two young sons that seemed to delight in the hip gadgetry of the Nova walkers. I decided to focus my attention on the boys, ages 8 and 10. They told me all about their grandfather and how badly he needed a walker. So, right there on the spot, I made them official walker experts.

I had fun showing them all the cool features available and how they contribute to independent living. Both boys responded enthusiastically. They were more convinced than ever that their grandfather would love having a walker. The best part for me was when they realized that a Mobility Makeover would also improve their lives. "Think of all the things grandpa can do with us when he gets his walker!"

I told the boys, "Okay, it's in your hands now. Here's your mission. Take this walker to your grandfather and tell him all the things you have planned to do together — if he'll only change his mind about having a new set of wheels."

The boys were so excited. They couldn't wait to get home. But not just to present the new walker to their grandfather. Since they were now official walker experts, they were also ready and eager to teach grandpa about all the inner-workings of his new ride.

The parents looked at me with a new light in their eyes. "You know what, I think this is going to work."

I asked for a full report, of course, and it came back better than expected. Grandpa not only accepted his new walker, he also embraced the love of his grandsons and their many adventures to come.

Mobility gift tips:

1. When giving a rolling walker as a gift, get a large bow and put it on the product. Also, be sure to attach cool accessories such as cup holders and bags. You can even do the gift trick. First, give a new fun cup or tumbler. Then, after that gift has been opened, say, "This is for THAT - your new ride!"

2. Give the gift of canes in a bouquet. That's right - like flowers. Get a nice long stem rose box and place a selection of canes in the box - like flowers. And don't forget the tissue and bow!

3. Make sure the recipient knows, this gift is not just for them, it's for all of you. The real gift is the ability to get out and enjoy life together again!

Chapter Nine:
Defining Life on Your Own Terms
The Nova Mission

When my mother, Arlene was diagnosed with Stage IV cancer in 2011, I was devastated. I felt helpless and scared. My mom is a superhero, my best friend, and so incredible...the rare person that can light up a room, take every project to a new creative level, and bring out the best in anyone. My usual joyous, hopeful view of life was suddenly infused with fear. Fear of the unknown, fear of change, fear of the future.

I realized that my reaction to this crisis was similar to what often happens to people who suddenly lose their mobility: The D-words invade and hamper the ability to make the best of a challenging situation.

Fortunately for me, even while fighting a dreaded disease (more D-words), my mother was a source of strength and inspiration. As I went about my business, I recalled the many times my mother would listen to my stories about my Nova work. I'd share my hopes, frustrations, dreams and, of course, confess my Walker Stalker activities. She was always rapt and intensely interested in whatever I had to say. And she would always respond the same way. "You need to write this down. You need to share these experiences and write a book. You can change the world."

Initially, I admit, I was skeptical. Me...write a book? I'm not a writer.

Then much to my surprise, while flying at 30,000 feet on my way to a Nova business meeting, I began to write. All those hours on an airplane that

I used to dismiss as wasted time became my writing oasis. I cherished the solitude. No longer was I distracted by calls, endless e-mails, life's demands.

As Confessions of a Walker Stalker began to take shape, I would think of my mother and how she defined her life. Regardless of what came her way, she clung to her faith and stayed strong. Even while she was a single parent in Taiwan while my father was in America preparing for our new life, she was strong and capable.

Even while traveling to American with two small children, taking care of my father through his 13-year battle with cancer, all while chauffeuring her three children to piano lessons, and waiting in line for my must have Duran Duran tickets and my younger sister's must have Cabbage Patch Kids, she did not give in to fear.

Even when she became a widow at 41, my mother brought love and strength to everything she did. Her example showed me that we must always push through our difficulties and strive to define life on our own terms — because it is the only life we have.

There were other people, too, that inspired me. And on one flight after another, I would think about all the people I had met over the years. Good people who allowed me into their lives — some for a few moments, others for years. People who shared their history, stories, families and, most of all, their wisdom. I learned so much from men and women, young and old, who shared their mobility struggles and dreams with me. Like my mother, they had also defined their lives on their own terms.

I listened, I learned, I transformed.

Just as we have the right to define our lives, we have the responsibility to define our mobility. But it is challenging. We must keep our unique spirit, powerful mind, and passionate soul active and alive by making choices that hold our independence in high regard. We must cherish our freedom. And we must not give in to social stereotypes and ignorance about aging and facing new challenges.

By taking control of our mobility, we acknowledge that as long as we are breathing and able, we have more discoveries and adventures ahead of us. And we bring all the zest, passion and wisdom of our past to fully embrace and enjoy our future.

But there is another reason I want you to live at the highest level possible. I need you.

I can't fulfill my Walker Stalker mission alone. I need help today, just as I needed help these 18 incredible years to build Nova into a trusted creator and advocate of independent-living products. Admittedly, this has been the most fun and glorious group effort. The Original Walker Stalkers, my great accomplices, are my Nova Family. My thanks and gratitude to all of them is eternal. (big hug!)

In general, "stalking" is thought to be a solitary, secretive activity. But this is not necessarily true. Walker Stalkers are part of a movement, a revolution that includes my entire industry, as well as:

- The entire national Nova network
- Family
- Friends
- Colleagues
- Customers
- Caregivers
- Healthcare professionals
- Non-profit organizations and....
- You!

We must enlist the effort of millions of Americans so that we can re-define and re-engage our great American Mobility Gene — and get everybody moving again!

The potential for mobilizing is unlimited. The good that will come of it may have a profound impact on this nation's productivity, prosperity, self-image and worldwide respect. When we can truly say that everyone — including the millions of people who require independent living assistance — is living life to the fullest in the land of the free and home of the brave, then we will have fulfilled Nova's great mission: Our mission is to change the world — everyday — everyway.

We are passionately committed to connecting human relationships and fulfilling human experiences by providing products and services that help fully realize the potential and possibilities of people with physical challenges.

The Walker Stalker Revolution continues to teach me many life lessons. The most important is this: giving is the ultimate human exchange. When we freely give to one another, we feel needed, we have real purpose, and we are making the world a better place. Best of all, those who give the most, receive the most.

Giving also protects us from the D-words. Depression, Denial, Discrimination and Disability. The reality is that as much time as we spend thinking about ourselves – what we want, what we need, what we don't have, what we might lose – that doesn't make us happy. We are happiest when we are thinking about and giving to others.

So, give freely and allow others to do the same, regardless of physical challenges. It is all part of the ultimate human exchange. And it is one of the most powerful ways to define life on your own terms.

Walker Stalker Confession:
I Won't Stop

I love being a Walker Stalker. It allows me to witness the amazing transformation that can occur when a person is empowered to feel whole again.

Together we are on a mission to rid our country of Dis-Ability, gray metal walkers with dirty tennis balls, and insidious epidemics, such as Cane-Liosis.

Our Walker Stalker journey is just the beginning of a nation-wide Mobility Makeover that promises to improve life for millions of people. Together we will make a difference every day, in every way. It all matters.

So, go out and walk. Go out and stalk. Go out and make the world a better place. Define it in your own terms and help others do the same...One step at a time.

Sue Chen
Founder, CEO

In addition to running a growing business, Sue Chen is a philanthropist, a classical music lover, an avid scuba diver and a spokesperson for protecting the world's oceans. Sue is a Director for NAWBO-LA (National Association of Women Business Owners), YPO member, Trustee of the California Lutheran University Board of Regents, President of Reef Check Foundation and Director of Shark Savers. In 2011 she helped successfully lobby the California legislature to protect endangered shark species, was a finalist for the prestigious Ernst and Young Entrepreneur of the Year Award, recipient of the Community Leadership Award from the President's Council on Fitness, Sports and Nutrition, her company was named Supplier of the Year by Amerisourcebergen for the second year in a row and most recently, she was named one of the ten Most Powerful Women Entrepreneurs in Fortune Magazine's Most Powerful Women Issue. She is proud to now add author to her list of accomplishments.

nova

www.NovaMedicalProducts.com

1-800-557-6682
Los Angeles • Chicago

.

www.ingramcontent.com/pod-product-compliance
Lightning Source LLC
Chambersburg PA
CBHW050601280326
41933CB00011B/1941